Poems Of The Heart

Poems Of The Heart

ANGELA HAYNES GAYLE
XULON PRESS

Xulon Press
2301 Lucien Way #415
Maitland, FL 32751
407.339.4217
www.xulonpress.com

© 2021 by Angela Haynes Gayle

All rights reserved solely by the author. The author guarantees all contents are original and do not infringe upon the legal rights of any other person or work. No part of this book may be reproduced in any form without the permission of the author. The views expressed in this book are not necessarily those of the publisher.

Paperback ISBN-13: 978-1-6628-0312-3

Ebook ISBN-13: 978-1-6628-0313-0

Introduction

Poems from the Heart is a book written between the ages of nineteen to twenty-five years old. Some of the poems are personal and some of them shed light on things that were going on in the world at that time. During this time, my life was spiraling out of control and I did not know which way to turn, but I remember what my mother told me when I left home. I remember she said when I got into this kind of situation to call on Jesus. My life was changed in an instant. Not only was I delivered, but my soul was set free. I owe it all to my mother for loving me enough to tell me about Christ Jesus. My hope is not only for this book to reach many, but that it may change the lives of many that it reaches.

Angela Hàynes Gayle

Table of Contents

Introduction v

A Friend 2
A Father's Love 3
Renewed Life 4
A Mother's Love 5
Hate 6
Different Lifestyles 7
Suicide 8
The Author Of Peace 9
Tomorrow 10
Foundation Of Love 11
Love Of The Church 12
Adults Immoral Disease Six 13
Believe In Yourself 14
Love Is... 15
Jesus Is My Lord 16
But Jesus 17
Grace 18
Things Will Come 19
An Expression Of Our Love To You 20
Crossroads 21
A Journey Toward Justice 22
If It Had Not Been For Calvary 23
The Price Is Right 24

About the Author 25

A Friend

A Friend is someone who you can trust in forever.
A Friend is someone that inspires your life.
A Friend is someone that you can talk with
And laugh with.
A Friend will be there in good times and sad times.
A Friend is someone who will stand beside you
And guide you.
A Friend will feel the pain you feel.
A Friend is someone of a free spirit, and someone whose love is real.

A Father's Love

A Father's love is one every child needs.
A Father's love is beyond demand.
A Father's love is teaching his children to understand.
A Father's
love will not let you down, but
He will always be there to help turn your life around.
A Father's love is to lead the family,
In truth and values of life.
A Father's love' comes without measures, or strife.

Renewed Life

Reflections Of An Alcoholic

To live as an alcoholic is not okay.
Trying to belong and hurting your loved ones,
      along the way.
To live a new life-style was what I wanted,
      but I knew drinking was
      not the solution, nor was
      it the way.
Drinking made me feel good, when I was rejected
      and felt out of place.
Since God has come unto my life, now I'm drunk
      Free; there is no more trying
      to belong to a society that
      once rejected me.
I'm bought with a price that I can never repay
      and I promise, still today,
      to take the love and strength
      He has given me and share it
      with the loved ones I hurt
      along the way.

A Mother's Love

A Mother's love goes beyond what our
      eyes can see, as she
      meets you with open arms,
      and gives you hugs and kisses
      as you grow along the way.

A Mother's love is patient, gentle, and free:
      giving of herself daily
      without asking for
      anything.

A Mother's love is a gift from God,
      because without it there
      would be no you or me.

A Mother's love prays for you and never
      gives up on you, as you
      travel life's journey along
      the way.

Hate

Hate is telling someone you hate him or her when you
    really don't know why.
Acting out shameful circumstances that have now
    became a lie.
Taking advantage of the people that love you,
    and pretending everything is fine, all
    because you don't want your so-called friends
    to leave you behind.
Even if it has taken you so long to realize what
    the cost of love can do, just remember you
    chose the love of friendship instead of
    the loved ones who cared and shared their lives
    with you.

Different Lifestyles

Why must I suffer and why do I feel alone? Has
Everyone rejected and forsaken me to live a
Lifestyle of their own?
There is no one to talk to and no one seems to care,
Just as long as they're happy getting and taking
Things that aren't really theirs!

The lifestyle I have with God is the best
Among all the rest; never wanting nor living with
Doubt, but always knowing His love will bring me out.

Always remember God has everything worked out, and
The awards He has for you in glory are the
Ones worth shouting about.

Suicide

Suicide: is it the only way out?
You say maybe if someone listened or lent you a little time, suicide wouldn't be your destiny, nor would it controls your mind.

Suicide: is not a cry for sympathy, nor is it a Joke; it's murder. People kill Themselves because they have lost all Hope, and they can no longer cope.

Suicide: is like AIDS; it has no specific color. It is the painful process of trying to die, except you decide when you want the pain to stop.

Suicide: is not the right choice to make; life is worth more than you can see. Just trust and hope for a better tomorrow, and each day you must believe that if you can cope with just one day, you will be surprised at what tomorrow will bring.

The Author Of Peace

Every morning I arise, I thank God for opening my
      eyes to another day.
As I open my patio door, I can feel the cool
      breeze, but only for a moment;
      then there is peace.
As I look out the sun shines so brightly, bringing
      glory upon the earth, but
      only for a moment; then there
      is peace.
I then listen as the birds also sing praises of
      thanks, but only for a moment;
      then there is peace.
The rain, which comes down, gives praise, with the drops
      of the same rhythm, but only
      for a moment; then there is peace.
The joy of knowing that every day will be different,
      but there is one thing you
      can count on: God will always
      give you peace.

Tomorrow

Tomorrow isn't ours to look forward to.

Tomorrow is something that is granted to us
    by God's grace.

You could close your eyes today without awaking
    tomorrow to see your loved one's face.

So slow down and enjoy each day you live, always
    thanking God for the love and strength
    He gives.

Every day is like being born over and over again.
    Enjoy the sunshine, fresh air, joy, and
    peace that each day will bring.

Foundation Of Love

Laying a foundation isn't easy, if you have the three main ingredients in order to have a solid surface.

If you start out with these ingredients, and you lose two along the way, your surface has lost its base.

If you don't have the Father, Son, and the Holy Ghost, your surface will not stand.

So you must have faith and trust, knowing that the foundation you lay will stand.

Love Of The Church

The church is the Bride of the living God, but
    Why are some of us so dead inside?
To know Him is to live, but to honor him
    is love.

So why do some Christians lie and steal from
    The person above, who we all
      proclaim to love?

If everything is His and nothing is ours, don't
    you think He will take care
    of those who is taking care
    of His sheep.

Some of us will continue to play,
    while those of us
      who love Him will receive awards
      and blessings.

The church of the living God, will there be one
    when He comes back?

Adults Immoral Disease Six
(AIDS)

AIDS are destroying this world; what is this lost
    generation going to do?
They say practice safe sex, and they leave that
    decision between you and me.
There is no such thing as safe sex, but there is
    a word we all know; and that
    the word is <u>no.</u>
Are sex and drugs so important that you make
    careless decisions that later
    destroys your life? Think twice
    before you throw your life and
    dreams away.
AIDS is not a gay thing, nor is it a black or white
    thing. AIDS is everybody's' problem;
    make the right choice.
    LIFE OR DEATH

Believe In Yourself

There are times when you will feel like quitting
    and giving up everything
    you are trying so hard to
    achieve.
There are hard times, good times, and bad times
    too.
If you hold on having faith and never
    look back and never want
    to stop.
There is a mountain in everybody's lives, but you
    must try hard to reach the top,
    and once you have gotten over,
    never forget who got you
    there.
Always believe in yourself and everything you do,
    having faith and trust, knowing
    that the Lord will see you
    through.

Love Is...

Love is the beginning of a new life.
Love is giving without, expecting anything
  back in return.
Love is being there for one another and
  taking care of each
  other.
Love is giving respect and honesty to one
  another.
Love is something that grows from within, and
  standing beside each other
  through thick and thin.
Love is never asking why or never giving in,
  but telling each other
  you love them and being a
  friend.

Jesus Is My Lord
(HE IS EVERYTHING TO ME)

Jesus is my Lord; it's His commands that I respond to. He has given me life. Once I was blind but now I see...**Jesus is Everything to Me.**

Using me as His tool for the whole world to see, blessed is He who believe that He died on Calvary to save the unrighteous like you and me.

I once was lost but now I'm found. My Lord is the reason that I'm standing on holy ground. Jesus is MY Lord. He has given me so much joy and love. He is everything to me...**Jesus is Everything to Me.**

But Jesus

No one knows the pain I feel: **But Jesus…**

No one knows the scars that are within: **But Jesus…**

No one can count my tears that fall: **But Jesus…**

No one can make my cloudy days into sunny days: **But Jesus…**

No one can really understand my ways: But Jesus…

He is the only person I strive and desire to be
like, because no one knows me better than **Jesus…**

Grace

We Are Blessed

We are blessed because grace has been extended to us. Our blessings are more than our eyes can see.

We are blessed because grace payed the price on Calvary. So we must seek Him now and just hold on, because just knowing grace will make you strong.

We are blessed because grace owns the world and no one should be lost. Count your blessings now or they soon will be cut off.

Things Will Come

The good things in life will come, but you must have patience and wait, no matter how long it takes.

Jesus, I know Him and I know He will make a way, if you trust and believe in Him today. Search and you will find that He is joy, love, peace, and truth. You must always have faith that God will see you through.

HE IS MY CAPTAIN IN THE MIDST OF THE STORM.

HE IS MY COUNSELOR WHEN I NEED SOMEONE TO TALK TO.

HE IS MY FRIEND WHEN I NEED SOMEONE TO LEAN ON AND WHEN I'M FEELING ALL A-LONE.

That is why I know good things will come. That's one thing I surely know, but you must be patient and wait, no matter how long it takes.

An Expression Of Our Love To You

Today is a special event;
One that we gladly
Share to show our pastor
And his family
How much we really care.
You have enlightened our lives.
In so many ways, we can't
Even begin to pay back
The love you gave.
You've been here for us
Through the hard times,
Bad times, and sad times too.
How gracious we are to God
For sending us a pastor
And family such as you.
"We Love You"
B.B.C. Family

Crossroads

At first when you started out, the road
seemed very long, but the
path in which you took made you
strong.

Now you've grown up and it's time
to move on.
It's time to face the world that awaits
you head on.

So, don't get discouraged but continue
to pray, because satan
has a roadblock along the way.

The crossroads ahead are already
paved, and God's blessings
for you are already laid. So make
sure you don't take
any detours, for it is written that
The victory is yours.

May God go with you as you journey
on, but remember all
things are possible; but you must believe and pray,
As you travel the crossroads along
the way.

A Journey Toward Justice

God sent His only begotten Son to take
our place for the wrong
we have done. He was a man who showed
compassion and perfection.
In all His ways none could find
fault in Him, not even till
this very day. But the people wanted
justice for what they
believed, so they sentenced the only
begotten Son to die on Calvary.
No one would stand for Him (my, I
wonder why?) Even the ones
who claimed they loved Him had just
denied Him twice and, as
He marched on the crowd, yelled, "Crucify,
crucify." He was stoned
and spit on, but yet He marched on
and how I thank God that
Justice stepped in, because the redemption
plan of our Savior freed the
world from all unrighteousness and sin.
On His journey toward
Justice, He had only us in mind. He loved us
that much that His perfectness
was His crime.

If It Had Not Been For Calvary

MATTHEW 27:28-35

Oh! Precious Lord, how I thank
thee for Your only
begotten Son, who hung, bleed, and
died for me on
Calvary.

But because He lives, I can now
testify of how His
goodness and grace has restored
my life.

If it had not been for Calvary,
where would You and
I be? All praises
To the Almighty
for taking our place on
Calvary.

The Price Is Right

If you're in need of healing and you
don't know which way to go,
God's calling your name so come on
down, seek His face,
while He can be found. Allow Jesus
Christ, the Savior, to turn your life around. Yes! The
price is right and the
gift is free, because the only begotten
Son died on Calvary.
The price is right and the way is
paved, so choose
ye the Lord on this day.

About the Author

Hi my name is Angela Haynes Gayle, I'm the daughter Of Mr. & Mrs. Haynes of Jewtt, Texas. After graduating high school, my life became a rollercoaster with highs and lows. In 1991 -2002, I began to write about things that had happened in my life and things I was dealing with in my life. Some 20 years later here I'm with my first book 'Poems from the Heart", writing was something I loved to do and being an author was something I always dreamed of becoming and well the rest is history. I hope that something I have written in this book changed someone's life.

www.ingramcontent.com/pod-product-compliance
Ingram Content Group UK Ltd.
Pitfield, Milton Keynes, MK11 3LW, UK
UKHW041957230426
12048UKWH00008B/386